LOST ISLAND ALPHABET

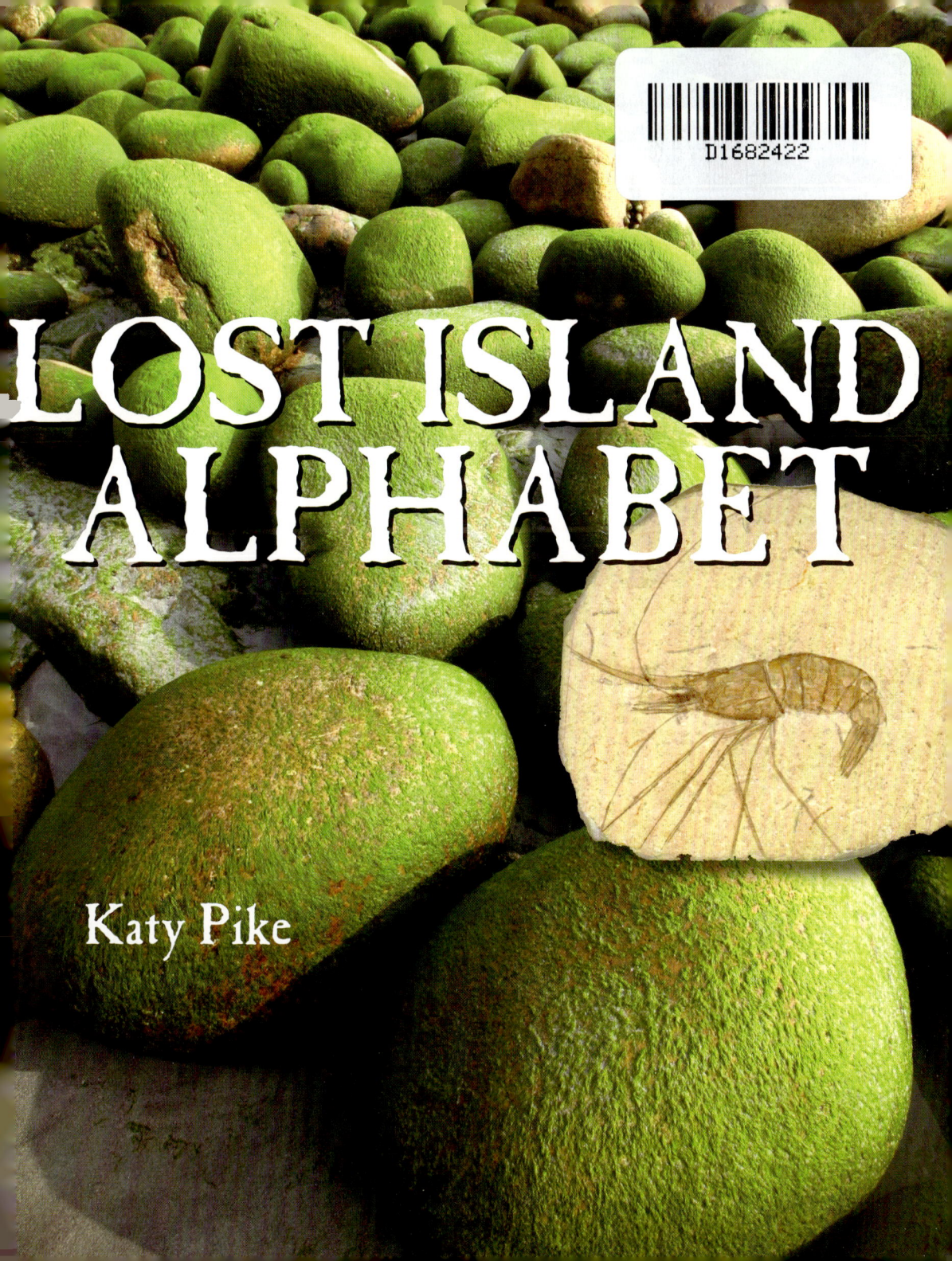

Katy Pike

Aa

alligator

Allosaurus

atoll

antenna

apricot

Bb

bone

bubbles

branch

beach

Brachiosaurus

3

Cc

climb

clouds

claw

coral

collection

Dd

dinosaur

dress

dive

dolphin

Diplodocus

Ee

eat

eel

Elasmosaurus

egg

ear

Ff

fruit

fossil

fairy

fish

flying

7

Gg

green

ground

game

Galapagos

garden

Hh

hawk

herd

howl

horn

helicopter

9

Ii

illustration

itch

island

iguana

ivy

10

Jj

jewels

jungle

jellyfish

juice

jump

11

Kk

kick

kitchen

kangaroo

koala

kettle

Ll

lake

laugh

lizard

legs

leaves

13

Mm

mushroom

mosquito

moss

mountain

mud

Nn

neck

night

nettle

nest

nectar

15

Oo

onion

otter

ocean

orangutan

octopus

Pp Qq

pink

purple

pixie

penguin

quince

17

Rr

rapids

ribs

raspberry

run

river

18

Ss

scales

sponge

swim

sea

sand

19

Ss

seaweed

Stegosaurus

seeds

spikes

shell

20

Tt

tree

tree house

Tyrannosaurus Rex

Triceratops

teeth

21

Uu Vv

vase

underwater

unlock

valley

vine

Ww

wood

wave

wild

wing

waterfall

23

Xx Yy Zz

Xenotarsosaurus

yellow

zebra finch

yabby

Zephyrosaurus